Heart of Darkness

Joseph Conrad

About this Book

For the Student

 Listen to the story and do some activities on your Audio CD

Talk about the story

tune When you see the orange dot you can check the word in the glossary

P Prepare for Cambridge English: Preliminary (PET) for Schools

For the Teacher

 A state-of-the-art interactive learning environment with 1000s of free online self-correcting activities for your chosen readers.

Go to our Readers Resource site for information on using readers and downloadable Resource Sheets, photocopiable Worksheets and Answer Keys. Plus free sample tracks from the story.
www.helblingreaders.com

For lots of great ideas on using Graded Readers consult Reading Matters, the Teacher's Guide to using Helbling Readers.

Level 5 Structures

Modal verb *would*	Non-defining relative clauses
I'd love to ...	Present perfect continuous
Future continuous	*Used to / would*
Future perfect	*Used to / used to doing*
Reported speech / verbs / questions	Second conditional
Past perfect	Expressing wishes and regrets
Defining relative clauses	

Structures from lower levels are also included

CONTENTS

HELBLING DIGITAL

e·ZONE
THE EDUCATIONAL PLATFORM

HELBLING e-zone is an inspiring new state-of-the-art, easy-to-use interactive learning environment.

The online self-correcting activities include:

- reading comprehension;
- listening comprehension;
- vocabulary;
- grammar;
- exam preparation.

🔲 **TEACHERS** register free of charge to set up classes and assign individual and class homework sets. Results are provided automatically once the deadline has been reached and detailed reports on performance are available at a click.

🔲 **STUDENTS** test their language skills in a stimulating interactive environment. All activities can be attempted as many times as necessary and full results and feedback are given as soon as the deadline has been reached. Single student access is also available.

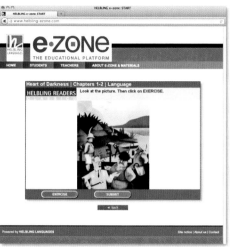

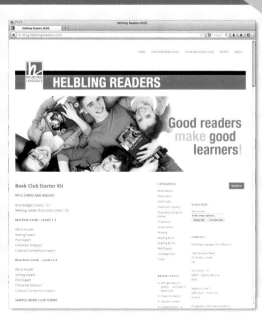

About the Author

Joseph Conrad was born in 1857, in Berdychiv, part of the Polish Ukraine. His real name was Jozef Teodor Konrad Nalecz Korzeniowski. Conrad lived in the Ukraine and Russia as a child and after the death of both of his parents, he was looked after by his uncle in Poland. From an early age he learnt French, read Shakespeare and became very fond of * the Polish romantic poets, but he also had a passion for the sea. His uncle allowed him to go to sea as soon as he had finished school and in 1878, he joined the British Merchant Navy, eventually becoming a captain. Conrad sailed extensively * all over the world and in 1890 he went to the Belgian Congo, which was later his inspiration for *Heart of Darkness* (1902). This journey, however, made Conrad ill and in 1894, he gave up the sea to become a full-time writer, mainly because of his health problems.

In 1886 Conrad obtained British nationality and when he left the navy he settled * in the south of England. In 1895, his first novel – *Almayer's Folly* *, an adventure set on the coast of Borneo – was published. In 1896 he married Jessie George and they had two sons. He regularly published short stories, novels and essays, but was not financially successful until 1913, when his novel *Chance* became popular. Conrad was widely recognised as a remarkable * writer by other writers, and his novels *Lord Jim* (1900), *Heart of Darkness* (1902), *Nostromo* (1904), *The Secret Agent* (1907) and *Under Western Eyes* (1911) were highly praised. His ability to handle * English with such style is even more impressive * when one thinks that it was his third language. Conrad died of a heart attack in 1924.

> ## Glossary
>
> * **extensively:** (here) a lot
> * **folly:** foolish or stupid action
> * **fond of:** attached to; liked
> * **handle:** use
>
> * **impressive:** that one admires
> * **remarkable:** extraordinary; very good
> * **settled:** went to live

About the Book

Heart of Darkness, like many of Joseph Conrad's novels, is based on his own experience as a sailor. This story is closely connected to the period that he spent working for a Belgian trading company* on a river steamer* on the Congo River, which he captained for a short time. He returned sick, and disillusioned with the Belgians' imperialistic attitude to the local people.

There are two narrators in *Heart of Darkness*: an anonymous* narrator on board the *Nellie* and Marlow. The first narrator starts the novel and then introduces Marlow, who then in turn tells his story. At the end of Marlow's story, the anonymous narrator then finishes the novel in his own words. This technique is called a frame narrative.

The main story in *Heart of Darkness* is the part narrated by the sailor Marlow. He tells some other sailors of his experience as the captain of a steamboat on a large river in Africa. Marlow's job is to transport ivory*, and then to go and bring back the company's best ivory agent – Mr Kurtz – who is believed to be sick. After a long delay because the boat has to be repaired, they sail up the river. They find Kurtz, who seems to have become a leader for the local people. Eventually, Marlow gets him onto the boat, but Kurtz dies on the way back down the river.

The word 'darkness' from the title has different symbolic meanings in the text: the jungle, evil, corruption and exploitation. And it seems that, in the end, Mr Kurtz has picked up* the 'darkness' rather than taking the 'light' to the people.

The novel is an attack on colonialism and imperialism, although it has been argued that Conrad dehumanises the Africans, making them no more than a part of the dark and dangerous jungle.

Heart of Darkness has been translated into many languages and adapted for radio and television. The most famous adaptation is Francis Ford Coppola's film *Apocalypse Now* (1979).

- **anonymous:** without a name
- **ivory:** hard white substance on elephants' tusks
- **picked up:** (here) been influenced by
- **steamer:** boat which moves by steam power
- **trading company:** company that buys and sells things

Before Reading

1 This story focuses on a journey along the Congo River, also known as the Zaire, in Africa in 1902.
Look at the pictures and words and then use them to complete these sentences from the story. Look up any words you don't know in a dictionary.

desolate natives journey steamboat wilderness canoe

a) We followed the coast of Africa which seemed like the edge of a ....

b) Kurtz's station was empty and .... in the heart of the jungle.

c) The .... ' camps surrounded the place, and the chiefs came to see him every day.

d) A lone white man paddling back in his .... with four natives.

e) But in order to understand the effect this .... had on me, you need to know a number of things.

f) I got a job with the company as the captain of a river ....

2 What do you know about the Congo River and the jungle surrounding it? Work with a partner and do some research on the internet.

3   The main character Marlow says: *'I remembered there was a foreign company that <u>traded</u> on the Congo River.'* Read this definition below.

trade: the action of buying and selling goods and services

In 1902 what goods were taken to Africa and what goods were brought back from Africa by traders? Fill in the lists below, choosing from these items.

BEADS

IVORY

COTTON

ALCOHOL

RUBBER

GOLD

Taken TO Africa	*Brought back FROM Africa*
....	....
....	....
....	....
....	....

4   Do you know which tragic form of trading once existed in Africa? Do some research on the internet if necessary.

Before Reading

1 **Marlow is the main character and the narrator of the story. Read the description of him and then tick (✓) the best ending to the sentence below.**

'Marlow was the only one of us who was still working as a sailor. He was a seaman and a wanderer. He was interested in the ships, the sea, the foreign ports that he visited and the foreign faces that he saw.'

Marlow is a typical seaman because:

a) ☐ he is curious and likes adventure.
b) ☐ he likes to spend time on his own.

2 **Listen to this text about Marlow and his new job and then tick (✓) the correct option.**

a) Marlow will be working for
   ☐ a Belgian company   ☐ a German company
   ☐ an English company
b) He will be travelling along the river in a
   ☐ canoe   ☐ cruise ship   ☐ steamboat
c) How does he feel about this new job?
   ☐ worried   ☐ depressed   ☐ excited
d) On his journey along the Congo River there will be
   ☐ three main stops   ☐ one stop   ☐ two small stops

3 **Listen to the text again and put the names of the stops of Marlow's journey in the correct order. Write 1, 2, 3.**

☐ Inner Station   ☐ Outer Station   ☐ Central Station

4 **Kurtz is the other main character in the novel. He is an ivory agent and a trader. Read the descriptions of him. Then match the words with their definitions.**

'… a first class agent and a very remarkable person.'

'Kurtz will go very far … He will become important in the administration before long.'

'A prodigy … next year he will be assistant manager.'

a) ☐ remarkable   1 to be successful
b) ☐ to go far   2 extraordinary
c) ☐ a prodigy   3 a talented person

5 **What type of job could a man like Kurtz do today? Discuss in class.**

6 **These are Marlow's thoughts about Kurtz. Complete the sentences with the words below.**

> imagine   desolate   natives   colleagues   canoe
> lone   headquarters   wilderness

'And for the first time I felt I could really a) .... what Kurtz was like. A b) .... white man, turning his back on the c) .... and his d) ...., and paddling back in his e) .... with four f) ...., to his empty and g) .... station in the h) ....'

7 **How does Marlow's image of Kurtz differ from the one in Exercise 4? Discuss with a partner.**

Chapter 1

 Night was falling. We were sitting on the *Nellie*, a sailing boat. We were anchored* in the Thames in London, waiting for the tide* to change so that we could leave. The air was dark, and there was a great gloom* all over the city. All five of us were experienced sailors and old friends, and we were relaxed together. As the darkness increased, we saw more and more lights on the small boats going backwards and forwards across the river.

'This* has also been one of the dark places of the earth,' said Marlow suddenly.

Marlow was the only one of us who was still working as a sailor.

He was a seaman, and also a wanderer*. He was interested in the ships, the sea, the foreign ports that he visited and the foreign faces that he saw. And he was also very interested in understanding deeper and more complex things about the places that he visited and the people that he met. So his remark* was not surprising to us, and nobody answered. Then he continued, very slowly:

'I was thinking of the very old times, when the Romans first came here*, nineteen hundred years ago. They sailed up the river Thames to a dark and wild place, with bad weather, bad food and death hiding all around them. But the Romans were strong enough to face the darkness. They were conquerors. They just took what they could get.

Glossary

- **anchored:** boat was fixed in one place with a heavy chain and object
- **gloom:** darkness
- **here:** (here) London
- **remark:** spoken opinion
- **this:** (here) London
- **tide:** rise and fall of the sea that happens twice a day
- **wanderer:** person who likes to travel and explore new places

Conquest is not a nice thing when you look at it too closely: it is robbery and murder on a large scale. Conquerors, of course have the idea that conquest is something noble, that has real meaning.'

Marlow broke off*. We watched the lights on the river, waiting patiently for him to continue. After a long silence, Marlow went on*, 'I once sailed up a big river,' and we knew that he wanted to tell us one of his long inconclusive* stories.

Marlow began his story.

I don't want to bother* you too much with what happened to me personally. But in order to understand the effect this journey had on me, you need to know a number of things: how I got there, what I saw, and how I went up that river to the place where I first met Kurtz.

A GOOD STORY
Which of these elements are important for you in a story? Tick (✓).
☐ Background and description.
☐ Good plot with lots of action.
☐ Satisfactory ending.
☐ Hidden meaning and moral.
☐ Convincing characters.

Glossary

* **bother:** annoy; tell
* **broke off:** (here) stopped speaking
* **inconclusive:** without a satisfactory end
* **went on:** continued

I was hanging around London, resting before looking for my next job. At first I wanted to go back to sea, but I couldn't find a ship. Then one day I saw a map in a shop window that I had seen as a boy. It was a map of a big dark area near the equator with a huge river in its centre. I decided that I wanted to go there: to Africa. I remembered there was a foreign company that traded * on the Congo River, and that I had an aunt who knew one of the bosses of that same company. And so thanks to my aunt I got a job with the company as the captain of a river steamboat *.

Within forty-eight hours I was crossing the Channel * to meet my employers in Belgium and sign the contract. While I was there I was also asked to have a medical * in which a little old doctor took my pulse * and measured my head. I thought this was strange and I asked him why this was important.

'The biggest change to the men who go to Africa happens inside their heads,' he said mysteriously. He then asked me if there was a history of madness in my family. This annoyed me greatly and I told him so.

'Just remember to avoid getting angry when you are out there. In the tropics *, anger can be more dangerous than the sun. Keep calm. Calm. Goodbye,' he said before signalling for me to leave.

Before starting my job I went to thank my aunt. She was very kind to me and she seemed to think I was some kind of 'taker of light', going out to Africa to help 'those ignorant millions change their horrible ways and bring them civilisation'. I reminded her, however, that I was actually going to work for a company that was interested in profit.

- **Channel:** sea between England and France
- **medical:** examination by a doctor to check you are healthy before you start a job
- **steamboat:** boat which moves by steam power
- **took my pulse:** counted my heartbeats
- **traded:** bought and sold things
- **tropics:** area near the equator

I felt that I was going, not to the centre of a continent, but to the centre of the earth.

CONQUEST / COLONISATION

Where is Marlow going?
What nationality is the company he now works for?

Marlow talks about the Roman conquest of Britain.
Look up the word 'conquest' in a dictionary.
Marlow decides to work for a European company that trades in Africa. What do you know about the European colonisation of Africa? Look up the word 'colonisation' in a dictionary.
What is the difference between conquest and colonisation?
Discuss in groups.

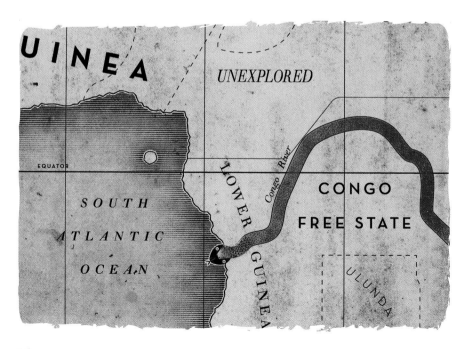

Chapter 2

I left in a French steamboat. We followed the coast of Africa which seemed like the edge* of a wilderness*. The dark green jungle was almost black beside the glittering* sea. Sometimes we saw black-skinned men paddling* a boat; they were a great comfort to look at, a momentary contact with reality. Once we came upon* a French ship, anchored off the coast, firing into the jungle with heavy guns for no apparent reason.

It was more than thirty days before we got to the mouth of the big river. I then changed boat and travelled up the river on a smaller steamer with a young Swedish captain. He told me that he had recently taken another Swedish sailor up the river, but he had killed himself on the way. When I asked why, he answered: 'Who knows? The sun was too much for him, or the country perhaps.'

At last we arrived at a place where the earth was all dug up, and a lot of people, mostly black and wearing skins*, were moving about like ants*. There were houses on a hill, and a jetty* projected into the river.

'There's your company's station,' said the Swedish captain, pointing to three wooden buildings on the rocky hill. 'I will send your things up. Goodbye.'

I walked up the path towards the station. The black workers were building a railway. There were pieces of broken machinery everywhere and rusty rails*. Every now and then the natives ran to take cover and an explosion shook the ground. These explosions seemed to be the only proper work that was going on.

Glossary

* **ants:**
* **came upon:** found
* **edge:** outside limit
* **glittering:** shining
* **jetty:** wooden structure built in water

* **paddling:** using a short pole to move a boat or a canoe
* **rusty rails:** old railway lines
* **skins:** skins of dead animals used for clothing
* **wilderness:** area of wild land

17

I saw dark shapes lying in the shade. I soon realised that they were exhausted workers who had come to escape the sun and were now waiting to die. They stared vacantly at nothing, lying in unnatural positions. I stood and looked at them in horror, then hurried away towards the station.

Near the buildings I met a white man, who I found out later was the company's chief accountant*. He seemed like a vision! He was immaculately dressed in white. He was wearing a clean shirt and necktie, jacket, white trousers and polished boots. His hair was parted neatly and brushed. I shook hands with him.

The accountant and his books* were in perfect order – he had trained a native woman to look after him and his clothes in the three years he had been there.

But everything else was disorganised – people, things, buildings. Strings* of natives arrived and departed. They took with them a stream* of rubbishy* cottons, beads and brass wire into the depths of the jungle, further down the river. In return they brought a precious trickle* of ivory to the station.

TRADE
What is the company trading in and where?
What do you know about this product and its trade?
Discuss in groups.

19

I had to spend ten days at this outer trading station, which seemed like an eternity. I spent some of the time in the accountant's hot wooden office. Here, he sat on a high stool at his desk and wrote numbers. It was he who first spoke to me of Kurtz.

One day he remarked*, without lifting his head, 'In the interior you will no doubt meet Kurtz.' On asking, I was told that Kurtz was a first-class* agent, and a very remarkable person. He was in charge of a very important trading-post*, in the true ivory country. He collected as much ivory as all the other agents put together. 'When you see Kurtz,' he went on, 'tell him from me that everything here is very satisfactory. I don't like to write to him because you never know who might get hold of* the letter at the Central Station.' He paused, looking at me for a moment. 'Oh, Kurtz will go very far,' he continued. 'He will become important in the administration before long. They – the bosses in Europe, you know – intend him to become important.'

CAREER
Why does the accountant think that Kurtz will go far?
What does the expression 'go far' mean for you?
Tell a friend.

Glossary

* **first-class:** (here) very good
* **get hold of:** take
* **trading-post:** place where goods are exchanged
* **remarked:** said

The next day I left the station, with a caravan* of sixty men, each with a massive load*, for the three-hundred mile* walk.

We went on a network of paths, through long grass, through burnt grass, through bushes, up and down stony hills in burning heat; and there was a great solitude. The population had long gone* and we passed through empty villages. I had a fat white companion who at first kept fainting* in the heat, so I had to shade him with my own coat. I couldn't help but ask why he had gone there. 'To make money, of course,' he replied. Then he got a fever and had to be carried, which caused arguments with the carriers because of his weight. After fifteen days, we arrived at the Central Station. It was on a backwater* of the big river, surrounded by scrub* and forest.

Another fat white man – one of several agents with long sticks who had come to examine me – told me that my steamer was at the bottom of the river. He said I should go and see the general manager immediately. Apparently, a volunteer captain had broken the bottom of the boat on some stones, and the steamer had sunk near the south bank*. The work of raising the boat out of the river and repairing it was to take me several months.

The manager was an unremarkable man to look at, with cold blue eyes. He was obeyed, but not out of love, fear or respect. It was more to do with the power he had gained by being there. He was a common trader who had managed to stay healthy for three years. This was very unusual out here. He was not good at organisation, initiative or order. That was obvious from things such as the terrible state of the station. He had no learning or intelligence. He kept the routine going, that was all.

- **backwater:** part of a river where the water does not flow
- **bank:** land on side of a river
- **caravan:** (here) group of people who travel together in dangerous places
- **fainting:** losing consciousness
- **load:** amount carried
- **long gone:** gone away a long time ago
- **mile:** 1 mile = 1.6 km
- **scrub:** short trees and plants

Despite my thirty-mile walk that morning, the manager started telling me things as soon as he saw me. The up-river station had to be relieved*. There had been many delays already. They did not know who was dead and who was alive, or how they were – and so on, and so on. There were rumours that a very important station was in danger, and that its chief, Kurtz, was ill. He was very worried. He asked how long it would take to get the boat repaired.

'How can I tell?' I said. 'I haven't even seen it yet – probably a few months.'

'Well, let's say three months,' he said. 'That should be enough time. Then you can travel up to Kurtz.'

I walked out of his hut*, muttering* to myself my opinion of him. He was an idiot. I took it back later, however, when it turned out that three months was exactly how long the work of repairing the boat required.

I went down to the river to see the boat the next day. I looked back at the station and saw the company's agents with their absurd long sticks walking around in the sunshine. The word 'ivory' rang in the air; it was whispered and sighed*. It was almost as if the agents were praying. I've never seen anything so unreal in my life. The only real thing, perhaps, was their desire to get appointed to a trading-post where ivory was to be found, so that they could earn percentages. And outside, the silent wilderness surrounding this activity seemed great and unbeatable, like evil or truth, waiting patiently for this invasion to disappear.

Glossary

- **hut:** small, simple building
- **muttering:** talking unclearly
- **relieved:** remove the people who work there because they have done something wrong
- **sighed:** said in a low, sad voice

A few days later I met the man who made bricks* – although he had no material to make bricks with, and therefore he did nothing, like the other agents. He invited me to his room to talk. I looked at a painting of a woman on the wall, and he said that Kurtz had painted it more than a year ago.

'Tell me, please,' I said, 'who is this Kurtz?'

'The chief of the Inner Station,' he answered. 'A prodigy*. Today he is the chief of the best station, next year he will be assistant manager, two years more and... But I expect you know what he will be. You are part of the new group. The same people who sent him recommended you. I know.'

What he said was so far from the truth that I nearly started laughing – my aunt's influential friends were producing some strange effects on others.

What I needed to do my job was rivets*. They had boxes of them down at the coast. But we had none here. We had metal plates for the repairs, but nothing to fasten* them with, so I could not get on with the work and close the hole in the boat. While we waited I had plenty of time to meditate on Kurtz. I wasn't very interested in him. Still, I was curious to see whether this man, who had come here with moral ideas of some sort, would climb to the top after all, and how he would set about* his work when he got there.

STATIONS
What do you notice about the different names for the stations?

Glossary

- **bricks:**
- **fasten:** fix
- **prodigy:** genius

- **rivets:**
- **set about:** do; start

Chapter 3

 One evening I was lying flat on the deck° of my steamboat when I overheard° the manager speaking to one of his colleagues about Kurtz.

I understood that Kurtz had asked to be sent to that particular station to show the administration what he could do. He had come three hundred miles down the river with his assistant and the ivory to the headquarters°. But Kurtz had then turned and gone back to his station, saying that he preferred to work alone.

The two men I overheard talking were amazed that anyone would have done that. And for the first time I felt I could really imagine what Kurtz was like. A lone white man, turning his back on the headquarters and his colleagues, and paddling back in his canoe with four natives, to his empty and desolate station in the wilderness. The assistant had told the manager that Kurtz had been very ill, and had only partly recovered. It seemed that there had been no other news since then, and that was nine months ago. And there had been no more ivory, either.

'It's not my fault!' said the manager at this point.

'Very sad,' said his fat colleague.

'And he was such a problem when he was here, too. He said things like: "Each station must be like a light on the road to better things. A centre for trade, of course, but also for improving the natives and instructing them." Imagine! And he wants to be a manager himself!'

- **deck:** (here) flat outside area on a boat
- **headquarters:** main offices of an organisation
- **overheard:** heard without their knowledge

Some time later, the fat trader I had travelled there with left the headquarters and went into the wilderness with his group, and we heard no more of them.

We were to leave soon, too, and go towards Kurtz's station. I was very excited at the thought of meeting Kurtz, although it actually took us two months from the day we left the headquarters until we came to the bank below Kurtz's station.

ANTICIPATION

Why do you think Marlow is excited to meet Kurtz? Have you ever heard so much about someone that you are excited to meet them?

Going up that river was like travelling back to the earliest beginnings of the world, when vegetation was everywhere on earth and big trees were kings. An empty river, a great silence, an impenetrable forest. The air was warm, thick and heavy. There was no pleasure to be had from the brilliant sunshine. The water just ran on, deserted, into the shadowy distance. On silvery sandbanks lay hippos and alligators, side by side. Often the river was broken up by a series of small islands, and it was difficult to find the main channel to sail along. I had to watch at all times, for fear of hitting the bottom of the steamboat on the banks that were hidden under the water.

And then there were the continual repairs that had to be made to broken steam pipes. I was so busy that I often forgot where I was, but I felt it all the same; I felt as if the mysterious stillness was watching me.

As well as the manager, I also had three or four of the white agents from headquarters on board, and there were about twenty cannibals as my crew*. They often had to jump out and help push and pull the boat along where the water was too shallow to sail. I also had a fireman. He was a native who had been trained to watch the water gauge*. He knew that if the level of water was too low, the boiler* might explode. So he sweated and watched the gauge fearfully.

Sometimes we came upon a small station where a few white men came rushing* out full of joy and surprise and welcome; then the word 'ivory' rang in the air before we went on again into the silence. The empty water and trees, trees, trees, millions of trees, enormous, huge and high. And the little steamboat crawling* through it all. It made you feel very small, very lost. Where the others imagined they were going to, I do not know. To some place where they expected to get something, I suppose. For me we were crawling towards Kurtz – exclusively, as we penetrated further and further into the heart of darkness.

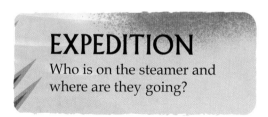

EXPEDITION
Who is on the steamer and where are they going?

Glossary

- **boiler:** (here) part of a steam engine where water is heated to provide power
- **crawling:** (here) moving slowly
- **crew:** people working on a boat
- **howled:** made a long, sad sound
- **reed-walled:** walls made of long grass
- **rushing:** running
- **water gauge:** instrument used to measure the amount of water present

It was very quiet, but at night sometimes there were drums from amongst the trees. The sound seemed to hang in the air above our heads until the first light of day. Nobody knew whether these drums meant war, peace or prayer.

Sometimes we found a native village, with reed-walled° houses with pointed grass roofs, and there was a sudden movement of black arms and legs, a mass of hands clapping, feet stamping and bodies moving on the bank. They howled° and leaped and spun, and made frightening faces. We sailed on past this incomprehensible display. We were cut off from any understanding of our surroundings. It was too distant from our everyday lives in the modern world. And yet, we could also relate to them and what they were doing, although it was remote from us. After all, they were human beings and so were we, and we all felt happiness, sadness, fear and anger in the same way.

HUMAN BEINGS

Do YOU prefer silence or noise?
Do YOU prefer stillness or movement?

29

About fifty miles below the Inner Station, we found a hut of reeds, a pole with a type of flag on top and a neat* pile* of cut wood. This was unexpected. I sailed close to the bank and on the pile of firewood someone had written: 'Wood for you. Hurry up. Approach cautiously.'

We were puzzled by the message. Where should we 'hurry up' to? Up the river? How could we 'approach cautiously' in a noisy steamboat? What was wrong higher up the river? And how bad was the situation? What a mystery!

As we travelled on, I expected the steamboat to stop working at any moment; however by the end of the second day from the hut we were about eight miles away from Kurtz's station. I wanted to continue, but the manager said that the river was very dangerous up there, and that it would be better to wait until morning. As we still had plenty of wood, I stopped the boat in the middle of the river for the night. It was in a straight stretch* of river with high trees on either bank. Everything was completely silent. And then night fell.

When the sun rose there was a white fog standing all around us, like something solid. It lifted briefly for a few minutes at around nine o'clock showing us the river, trees and sun, but then came down again, hiding everything. Suddenly the silence was broken; a very loud cry filled the air. This was followed by the noise of many voices shouting together in a desperate, complaining way. Then there was a series of dramatic cries. They seemed to come from all sides at once, but then they stopped as suddenly as they had started. The men from headquarters rushed out of the cabins with their Winchester rifles* ready...but ready for what? All we could see was the steamer we were standing on. The rest of the world had disappeared.

/ Glossary

- **neat:** tidy
- **pile:** amount of
- **stretch:** (here) part
- **Winchester rifles:** type of long guns

Chapter 4

I ordered the chain to be pulled up so that the anchor could be lifted easily and we could move if the fog cleared again.

'Will they attack?' whispered the frightened voice of a short fat man from headquarters.

'We will all be killed in this fog,' replied another.

The leader of the cannibals stood near me as his men pulled up the chain.

'Catch them,' he said to me. 'Catch them and give them to us.'

'To you?' I asked. 'What would you do with them?'

'Eat them,' he replied, looking out into the fog.

Of course, I realised, he and his cannibal friends were hungry! They had only eaten some dead hippo meat they had brought with them when we started over a month ago. We hadn't stopped as planned for them to get more food on the way. They had each been given three pieces of brass wire about 20 cm long every week; the theory was that they would buy their food with that currency in riverside villages. But that didn't work because there were either no villages, or the people were too hostile, or the manager didn't want to stop the boat for reasons of his own. Apart from the hippo, the only other thing I saw them eat was something which looked like half-cooked bread which they kept wrapped in leaves. Now that I think of it, I don't know why the thirty of them hadn't killed the five of us whites and eaten us!

CANNIBALS
What do you know about cannibals?
Do some research on the internet and discuss in groups.

'It is very serious,' said the manager's voice behind me. 'If anything happens to Kurtz before we get to him, I will be devastated.'

Despite what I had heard him say earlier as I lay on the deck of the steamboat, I believed he was being sincere. He was the kind of man who wanted to keep up appearances.

'We need to continue immediately,' he said.

I didn't bother to answer him as we both knew that it was impossible.

'I authorise you to take all risks,' he said after a short silence.

'And I refuse to take any risks,' I answered shortly.

'Well, I must accept your judgement. You are the captain,' he said in a surprisingly polite way. 'Will they attack, do you think?'

I did not think they would attack, for several obvious reasons. One, for the thick fog: if they left the bank in their canoes they would get lost in it, just as we would if we tried to move. Two, I believed that the jungle on either bank was impenetrable, even though there were eyes in it, eyes that had seen us. Three, during the few minutes that the fog had lifted, I had not seen any canoes anywhere.

But why I really thought they wouldn't attack was because of the *nature* of the sound they had made: it had given an impression of great sadness; the sight of our steamboat had filled these people with sorrow for some reason.

GUESS

Why do you think the sight of the steamboat has made the natives sad?

Eventually the fog lifted, and we steamed up the river until we were about a mile from Kurtz's station. There was a point in the river where we had to sail very close to the bank. Some of the trees and bushes hung over the water. From my cabin on the deck I was watching everything very carefully. At the front of the ship one of the crew was checking the depth of the water with a pole; below me the fireman was putting wood into the furnace*; and by my side the helmsman* was steering* the boat. All of a sudden the man at the front lay down on the deck, and the fireman bent down. I was amazed.

Then I looked up and I saw that the air was full of wooden sticks flying towards us. All this time the river, the bank and the woods were very quiet, so I could hear the noise of the engine and then suddenly the patter* of the arrows falling everywhere. Arrows! Someone was shooting at us!

I stepped into the cabin quickly and went to close the shutters* on the land side. Amongst the leaves I saw faces looking at me very fiercely and steadily, and as I looked more carefully I saw that the forest was full of people. And the arrows flew from them towards us. Below me on the deck the men from headquarters ran out with their Winchesters and shot into the bushes. The whole scene became confused, as smoke rose from the guns.

The helmsman grabbed the rifle in the cabin, opened the shutters I had closed, and shot into the trees, but this was a mistake because somebody threw or pushed a spear into his side below his ribs. He sank to the floor, crying in pain.

There was more shooting from the guns on the deck and wild screaming from the men in the jungle. I took over steering the ship, and grabbed the steam whistle* letting out a series of loud screeches*. The screaming in the forest stopped, and was followed by a long wail* of fear and sadness; it seemed as if the last hope had disappeared from earth. There was a great deal of movement in the bushes, and the shower of arrows stopped.

One of the agents from headquarters came up with a message from the manager, but I ignored him and made him steer the ship. He looked at the helmsman on the floor.

'He is dead,' he said quietly.

'No doubt about it,' I replied. 'And I suppose Mr Kurtz is dead as well by this time.'

I felt an extreme sense of disappointment. After this attack I was sure that Kurtz was already dead. I realised that I had come all this way to hear him speak, and that now I never would. It was not that he had managed to get more ivory than all the other agents together. The point was that he was a very gifted man, and that his most important gift was his ability to talk – that he could express himself like a stream of light. I thought, 'Good Lord! It's all over. We are too late; he has vanished – the gift has vanished – he has been killed. I will never hear him speak after all.' Of course, I was wrong. The privilege of listening to him was waiting for me. Oh, yes. And I heard more than enough.

Glossary
- **screeches:** high sounds
- **wail:** cry
- **whistle:** device used to make a high warning sound

When we arrived at Kurtz's hut, we found piles of ivory. We filled the steamboat with it, putting a lot of it on the deck. It was his. Everything was his. Kurtz talked like that: 'My ivory, my station, my river, my Intended*, my…' Everything belonged to him – but the thing I wanted to know was what he belonged to – what powers of darkness had taken him? What had changed him? Kurtz was obviously no longer the man I had heard about.

And Kurtz told me a lot before he died. This was because he was happy to speak English again after being alone with the natives for so long. He also showed me a report he had written on how the cruel traditions of the African natives could be stopped, 'The Suppression* of Savage Customs'. This report was seventeen pages of writing. (I have to point out that he had completed this report before his – let us say – nerves, went wrong and he started to take part in certain midnight dances that ended with the most terrible ceremonies.) When I read the report, I was impressed by the way it was written – his language was eloquent* and his words noble and passionate. But the whole thing led to a terrible conclusion: the only way to stop the traditions was to exterminate all the natives!

He begged* me to take good care of his report.

POWERS OF DARKNESS
What do you think went wrong for Kurtz?
What do you think the darkness represents?

---

* **begged:** asked; made a strong and urgent request
* **eloquent:** powerful and clear

* **Intended:** (here) woman he planned to marry
* **suppression:** stopping by force

But I am jumping ahead in my story. After the attack, we sailed the short distance to the station where we were met by a white man wearing brightly patched clothes. He came on board the steamboat.

'I don't like this,' I said to the man. 'The natives are in the jungle.'

'They are simple people,' he said. 'I am glad you came. It took me all my time to keep them away.'

He then started talking quickly about the boat and the people, as if he hadn't talked to anyone for a long time.

'Don't you talk to Kurtz?' I asked.

'You don't talk to that man,' he replied. 'You listen to him.'

I then asked him to tell me about himself. He was a Russian sailor, and had been sent into the jungle by a Dutch trading company. He explained that the house where we had found the wood had been his.

'I had lots of trouble to keep these people away,' he said.

'Did they want to kill you?' I asked.

'Oh, no!' he cried.

'Why did they attack us?' I continued.

'They don't want Kurtz to go,' he answered after a pause.

'Don't they?' I said curiously. And he nodded a mysterious nod.

'I tell you – this man has enlarged my mind,' he said, opening his arms wide.

Chapter 5

I looked at the Russian in his colourful clothes, and wondered how he had existed, how he had succeeded in coming so far down the river and how he had managed to remain here.

'I went a little farther,' he said, 'and then a little farther – till I had gone so far that I don't know how to get back. Never mind. Plenty of time. I can manage. You take Kurtz away quickly – quickly, I tell you!'

He told me about his time with Kurtz. I suppose that Kurtz wanted an audience, because one time when they had camped together in the forest, they had talked all night, or more probably Kurtz had talked.

'We talked about everything,' he said, excited by his memories. 'I forgot there was such a thing as sleep. Everything! Of love, too. He made me see things.'

'And have you been with him ever since?' I asked.

'No, he likes to wander alone and he often goes off into the depths of the forest,' he replied.

'Does he go exploring?' I asked.

He told me that Kurtz had discovered lots of villages, a lake, too – he did not know exactly in what directions – but that his expeditions had been for ivory.

'To speak plainly, he raided* the country,' I suggested.

He nodded.

'Not alone, surely?' I asked. 'Kurtz got the tribe to follow him, didn't he?'

Glossary

* **raided:** made a short sudden attack; (here) entered by force in order to steal the ivory

40

'They adored him,' he said. By the way that he said this, I could see that Kurtz filled his life, occupied his thoughts, changed his emotions.

'What can you expect?' he shouted. 'He came to them with thunder and lightning – his guns. They had never seen anything like it. He could be very terrible. You can't judge Kurtz as you would an ordinary man. No, no, no! He said he would shoot me unless I gave him my ivory because nothing could stop him from doing as he pleased. And that was true, too. I gave him the ivory. What did I care? But I didn't leave. No, no. I couldn't leave him. I had to be careful, of course, until we got friendly again. He was living for the most part in those villages by the lake. When he came down to the river, sometimes he got angry with me, and it was better for me to be careful. This man suffered too much. He hated this place, but he couldn't get away. When I had a chance, I begged him to try and leave while there was time; I offered to go back with him. And he said yes, and then he remained to go off on another ivory hunt, or disappear for weeks and forget himself amongst these people.'

'Why, he's mad!' I said.

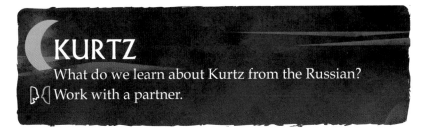

KURTZ

What do we learn about Kurtz from the Russian?
Work with a partner.

He protested strongly. Kurtz couldn't be mad. He was such a great talker and was a brilliant man. But it appeared, from what the Russian said, that Kurtz's appetite for more ivory had gradually changed his view of what was the right or wrong way to get it.

The Russian then explained that Kurtz had suddenly become quite ill. 'I heard he was lying helpless, and so I came up here – I took my chance,' he said. 'Oh, he is bad, very bad.'

There were no signs of life up at Kurtz's house on the hill, with its ruined roof, long mud wall and three little square windows of different sizes. I looked at it again through my telescope, and saw something which shocked me.

The top of each post in the fence around the buildings had the remains of a human head on it. I realised that these heads showed that Kurtz had a lack of restraint*, that he would do anything when he needed to. His morality and vision had been lost in the wilderness.

The Russian told me that he did not dare* to take the heads down. He was not afraid of the natives; they never did anything until Kurtz gave the word. Kurtz's power was extraordinary. The natives' camps surrounded the place, and the chiefs came to see him every day. He started to describe how they approached Kurtz, but I stopped him.

'I don't want to know anything about the ceremonies used when approaching Kurtz,' I shouted. I somehow found such details more unacceptable than the heads drying on the fence posts. The Russian seemed surprised by my attitude towards Kurtz.

Glossary

- **dare:** be brave enough
- **restraint:** self control

'I don't understand,' the Russian said. 'I've been doing my best to keep him alive. I have nothing to do with the heads – they were rebels – or the ceremonies. There has been no medicine or decent food here for months. Kurtz was shamefully* abandoned. A man like this, with such ideas…'

Suddenly round the corner of Kurtz's house a group of men appeared, walking through the tall grass and carrying a stretcher*. Instantly, there was a loud cry which cut through the air like a sharp arrow. As if by magic, streams of people appeared, with spears in their hands, with bows, with shields and with wild glances* and violent looks. They poured into the open area below the house, and then everything was still.

'Now if Kurtz doesn't say the right thing to them we are all finished,' said the Russian, who was watching by my side. The men carrying the stretcher stopped halfway towards the steamer where we were, and the man lying on it sat up.

'Let us hope that the man who can talk so well of love will find a good reason to save us,' I said.

I looked through my telescope and saw Kurtz with his thin arm held up above him commandingly, his mouth moving in speech, though we could hear nothing. He fell back suddenly, and the men with the stretcher moved forward again. At the same time, I noticed that the crowds were vanishing back into the forest as quickly as they had appeared.

* **glances:** quick looks   * **stretcher:**
* **shamefully:** terribly; deserving blame

Some of the men from headquarters were walking behind the stretcher carrying Kurtz's guns. The manager was walking beside the stretcher, talking to him. They laid him down in one of the little cabins on the steamboat which had just enough room for the bed and two small camp stools. We had brought his correspondence, and the bed was covered with many open letters and papers. He held up one of the letters and looked straight at me, saying: 'I am glad'. Someone had obviously written to him about me. I was struck by his voice, which was serious, deep and full, while he looked so ill and incapable of more than a whisper!

EXPECTATIONS

Marlow still hasn't 'met' Kurtz but he already knows a lot about him.
Have you ever known a lot about someone before you actually met them?
Did that person fulfil your expectations or were they very different from how you imagined them to be?

The manager appeared in the doorway and I stepped out to where the Russian and the men from headquarters were standing. I followed the direction that they were looking in. Dark, human shapes were visible, moving around the gloomy edges of the forest.

Near the river stood two bronze figures, leaning on tall spears and wearing fantastic head-dresses of spotted skins, warlike and quiet at the same time. And from right to left along the sunny bank, moved a wild and gorgeous woman.

She walked in a slow and proud way, jingling with metal ornaments at each step. She held her head high; her hair was done into the shape of a helmet; she had brass leggings to her knee, brass gloves to her elbow, and dark red spots on each cheek. Around her neck were many necklaces with glass beads that shook and glittered at every step. She was savage and superb and there was something dangerous in her slow, continuous movements.

She came to the side of the steamer, stood still and faced us. Her face had a mixture of sadness, fear and pain.

There was a terrible silence around us.

Then she turned away slowly and walked on, following the river bank, only turning once to stare at us for a moment, before she disappeared into the forest.

'If she had tried to come on board,' said the Russian, 'I think I would have shot her. I have been risking my life every day for the last fortnight to keep her out of the house. She got in one time and talked loudly to Kurtz for an hour, turning and pointing at me frequently. I don't understand the dialect of this tribe. Luckily for me, Kurtz was too ill to care that day, or I think I would have been in trouble. I don't understand. It's too much for me. Ah, well, it's all over now.'

At that moment I heard Kurtz's deep voice from the cabin.

'Save me! Save the ivory, you mean. Don't talk about saving me when I've had to save you! You are interrupting my plans now. Sick? Not so sick as you would like to think. Never mind*. I'll continue with my plans – I will return. I'll show you what can be done. You with your small business ideas – you are interfering with me. I will return.'

The manager came out. He took my arm and we walked to the side of the boat.

'He is very low,' he said. 'We have done all we could for him, haven't we? But you cannot hide the fact that Kurtz has done more harm* than good for the company. He was too aggressive in his work. Carefully, slowly, that's my way. We must be careful. This district is closed to us for a time. I don't say that there isn't a remarkable quantity of ivory, and we must save it all. But look how dangerous the situation is – and why? Because his method was not good. He has no judgement. I will have to make a report about it to the company directors.'

Glossary

- **done more harm:** created more problems
- **never mind:** don't worry

'Nevertheless*,' I said, 'I think Kurtz is a remarkable man.'

'He *was*,' answered the manager, and he walked away from me. He obviously thought I was as bad as Kurtz, and believed in methods which were not good. I was on the wrong side*.

The Russian tapped* me on the shoulder.

'I think these white men do not like me,' he said.

'You're right', I replied. 'Perhaps you had better go if you have any friends amongst these native people.'

'Plenty,' he replied. 'They are simple people – and I don't want anything from them. But I don't want anything to happen to these white men, and I am worried about Kurtz's reputation. I only told you what I did because we are both sailors.'

'All right,' I said, after a time. 'Kurtz's reputation is safe with me.'

He then told me in a low voice that it was Kurtz who had ordered the attack to be made on the steamer.

'He hated the idea of being taken away from here,' he went on. 'He wanted to scare you away. I could not stop him. Oh, I had an awful time this last month.'

'Thanks,' I said. 'I shall keep my eyes open.'

'I have a canoe and three natives waiting not very far away. I am going. Could you give me some cartridges* for my gun, please? And a pair of shoes.'

I gave him the cartridges and found an old pair of shoes for him.

'Ah! I'll never, ever meet such a man again. You should have heard him recite poetry – it was his own, he told me. Poetry! Oh, he enlarged my mind.'

'Goodbye,' I said. We shook hands and he vanished into the night.

- **cartridges:** ammunition used to fire a gun
- **nevertheless:** but
- **tapped:** touched lightly
- **wrong side:** (here) supporting the wrong people and opinions

Chapter 6

When I woke up just after midnight, I could see a big fire burning on the hill near the house, and other flames flickered* in the forest where Kurtz's adorers were waiting. I could hear the slow beating of a drum and the chanting* of many voices. I glanced into the little cabin. A light was burning, but Kurtz was not there. I didn't believe it at first – it seemed impossible. I realised that this meant we might be attacked at any moment, but I didn't raise the alarm, or tell any of the company agents who were sleeping on the deck. It had become my job not to betray Kurtz. I had made my choice and chose the nightmare of being on his side.

I got down off the steamer and onto the bank and saw a trail* through the long grass; it was obvious that Kurtz was crawling away. I eventually found him. He got up – long, pale and unsteady*.

'Go away – hide yourself,' he said in his deep voice.

'Do you know what you are doing?' I whispered.

'Perfectly,' he answered, raising his voice.

'You will be lost,' I said. 'Completely lost.'

'I had immense plans,' he muttered. 'I was going to do great things. And now because of this stupid manager…'

'Your success in Europe is certain, whatever happens,' I said, trying to appeal to something that was important to him. I knew that there was nothing above or below him. Kurtz was alone. I watched as he struggled with his own desires and hopes. I realised the terrible danger, because he could easily call the natives to kill us all. I had tried to break the spell of the wilderness that seemed to hold him so tightly.

Glossary

- **chanting:** repeating a word or phrase continuously
- **flickered:** moved
- **inconceivable:** impossible to understand
- **trail:** tracks
- **unsteady:** not balanced

Believe me or not, his intelligence was perfectly clear – concentrated, it is true, upon himself with horrible intensity, yet clear. This was my only chance: to appeal to his intelligence. (The other option was to kill him there and then, which wasn't so good, because of the noise it would make.)

But his soul was mad. Being alone in the wilderness, it had looked within itself, and, by heavens! I tell you, it had gone mad. And now it was my turn to look into his soul, too. He was eloquent and sincere until the end. He struggled with himself, too. I saw it, I heard it. I saw the inconceivable* mystery of a soul that knew no restraint, no faith, and no fear, yet struggled blindly with itself.

And finally, I helped him, his thin arm round my neck, back to the steamer.

We left the next day at noon. The natives came running out of the woods again and filled the area below the house on the hill. Two thousand eyes watched the steamer. Three men covered in bright red mud, with horned heads, walked up and down in front of the crowd of people, stamping their feet and shaking black feathers at us. They shouted and the crowd chanted replies. Kurtz watched from the couch in my captain's cabin. Suddenly the woman with the helmet of hair ran to the very edge of the river. She put out her hands and shouted something, and everyone took up the shout in a roaring chorus.

'Do you understand this?' I asked.

He kept looking out past me with fiery, longing eyes, with a mixed expression of wanting and hate.

'I certainly do,' he said slowly, with a small, meaningful smile on his lips.

I pulled the string of the whistle, because I saw the agents from headquarters getting their guns out. At the sudden screech there was a movement of complete terror amongst the huge crowd. I blew it again and again, and they ran away, twisting and turning. The three men in red fell down on the bank, face down, as if they had been killed. Only the wild and proud woman did not move, stretching her arms after us over the shining river.

The brown current ran out of the heart of darkness, carrying us down towards the sea with twice the speed of our upward progress; and Kurtz's life was running swiftly, too, flowing out of his heart into the sea of time. The manager was very quiet; he felt that things had ended as he wanted.

Kurtz talked. A voice! A voice! It rang deep to the very end. His brain was full of shadowy images now – images of wealth and fame. He spoke of 'my Intended, my station, my career, my ideas'.

The steamer broke down – as I had expected – and we had to wait for repairs by a small island. This delay shook Kurtz's confidence.

One morning he gave me a packet of papers and a photograph tied together with a shoelace. 'Keep this for me,' he said. 'This fool (meaning the manager) is capable of looking in my boxes when I am not there.'

I didn't have much time for Kurtz just then because I was helping to repair the engine. One evening when I came in with a candle I was surprised to hear him say: 'I am lying here waiting for death.'

'Oh, nonsense!' I replied.

His face changed, and I saw expressions of pride, power, terror – of an intense and hopeless despair. Did he live his life again in that moment? He cried out twice, a cry that was no more than a breath:

'The horror! The horror!'

I blew the candle out and left the cabin. I went to join the colleagues from headquarters for dinner. Suddenly the manager's boy put his head round the door and said: 'Mister Kurtz – he dead.'

Everyone else rushed to see, while I went on with my dinner. However, I didn't eat much. There was a lamp in there and outside it was so terribly dark. I didn't go near the remarkable man again. The next day the agents buried him in a muddy hole. The voice was gone. But I remained to dream the nightmare out to the end, and to show my loyalty to Kurtz once more.

Destiny. My destiny! He was a remarkable man. He had something to say. He had seen much, his stare was wide enough to take in the whole universe, and sharp enough to penetrate all the hearts that beat in the darkness. He had summed it all up* – he had judged. 'The horror!' His cry was an affirmation*, a moral victory paid for by many defeats, by horrible fears, by terrible satisfactions. But it was a victory! That is why I have remained loyal to Kurtz to the last.

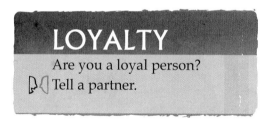

LOYALTY
Are you a loyal person?
Tell a partner.

Glossary

* **affirmation:** positive statement

* **summed it up:** given a summary; described the central idea in few words

Back in London, I found the daily life of ordinary people ridiculous, after what I had experienced. I kept the packet of papers given me by Kurtz, not knowing exactly what to do with it.

I was approached by a man from the company, who said they had the right to the papers. I gave him the report on the 'Suppression of Savage Customs' to read, but after glancing at it, he said that was not what he had expected. He left, and I didn't see him again.

Someone who called himself Kurtz's cousin appeared two days later, and told me that Kurtz had essentially been a great musician. I had never been able to decide what profession Kurtz had: a painter, a journalist? But we both agreed that he was a universal genius. I gave the old man some unimportant family letters and he left happily.

Finally a journalist came, asking to know something of the fate of his 'dear colleague'. He told me he thought that Kurtz was not a good writer.

'But heavens! How that man could talk. He electrified large meetings. He had the faith, you see. He could get himself to believe anything. He would have been an excellent leader of an extreme political party.'

'Which party?' I asked.

'Any party,' answered the man. 'He was an extremist, wasn't he?'

I agreed. I gave him the report to publish if he felt it was worth it, and he left contented.

KURTZ

Make a list of all the different things Kurtz could do.

So in the end I was left with a slim* packet of letters and the girl's portrait. I thought she had a beautiful expression. I decided I would go and give her the letters and portrait. I felt that everything that had been Kurtz's had passed out of my hands: his soul, his body, his station, his ivory, his career. There remained only his memory and his Intended. So I went to see her.

As I walked to the house I had Kurtz before me, as usual. Visions of him on the stretcher, the wild crowd of adoring natives, the gloom of the forests, the river, and the beat of the drums, regular as a beating heart – the heart of a victorious darkness. And the memory of what I had heard him say went with me, too. I remembered his pleading*, his threats*, his huge desires, his meanness, and the pain in his soul. As I rang the bell of the door, he seemed to stare out of it at me, that wide stare that accepted and hated all the universe. I seemed to hear his whispered cry: 'The horror! The horror!'

I waited in a large sitting room with three long windows from floor to ceiling. There was a tall, cold marble fireplace and a massive grand piano in the corner. A high door opened and closed. I stood up.

She came forward, all in black, with a pale head. She was in mourning*.

It was more than a year since his death, but she seemed as if she wanted to remember and mourn forever. Her eyes looked out at me with great depth, confidence and trustfulness. But as we shook hands, I saw an expression of great desolation come upon her face. For her, he had only died this minute.

Glossary

- **mourning:** being sad because of someone's death
- **pleading:** begging; urgent requests
- **slim:** thin
- **threats:** suggestions that something bad or violent will happen

We sat down and I laid the packet gently on a little table. She put her hand over it.

'You knew him well,' she murmured.

'Intimacy grows quickly out there,' I said. 'I knew him as well as it is possible for one man to know another.'

'And you admired him,' she said. 'It was impossible to know him and not to admire him.'

'He was a remarkable man,' I replied. 'It was impossible not to…'

'Love him,' she finished quickly, silencing me. 'How true! But no one knew him so well as I! I knew him best.'

The room was growing darker, but her forehead, smooth and white, remained illuminated by her eternal light of belief and love.

'You were his friend,' she went on. 'You must have been if he gave you this and sent you to me. I feel I can speak to you. Oh, I must speak to you. I want you – you who heard his last words – to know I have been worthy of • him.'

I listened. It grew darker. She talked as thirsty men drink.

'Who was not his friend who heard him speak?' she continued. 'He was able to bring out the best in people that he met. It is the gift of great men. But you have heard him! You know!'

'Yes, I know,' I said

'What a loss to me – to us – to the world.' I could see her eyes were full of tears that would not fall. 'I have been very happy – very fortunate – very proud,' she went on. 'Too fortunate. Too happy for a little while. And now I am unhappy – for life. And all of his promise, his greatness, his generous mind, his noble heart, nothing remains – nothing but a memory. You and I – '

'We shall always remember him,' I said quickly.

Glossary

• **worthy of:** good enough for

ADMIRATION
Why do you think Kurtz was loved and admired by so many different people and for so many different reasons?

'And his words will remain,' she said. 'And his example. Men looked up to him – his goodness shone in every act he did. I cannot believe that I shall never see him again, that nobody will see him again, never, never, never.'

She put out her arms as if somebody were leaving. Never see him! I saw him clearly enough then. I shall see his eloquent phantom* as long as I live.

'You were with him – to the last?'

'To the very end,' I said, shakily. 'I heard his very last words...' I stopped in fright.

'Repeat them,' she murmured in a heart-broken tone. 'I want something to live with.'

It was getting dark now and the darkness seemed to be repeating, 'The horror! The horror!'

'His last words. To live with,' she insisted. 'Don't you understand I loved him – I loved him!'

I concentrated and spoke slowly.

'The last word he pronounced was – your name.'

I heard a short sigh. Then there was a loud and terrible cry of unbelievable triumph* and terrible pain.

---

* **phantom:** ghost

* **triumph:** victory; when you win

'I knew it,' she said. 'I was sure!'

She knew. She was sure. She hid her face in her hands and wept. Kurtz always said he wanted justice. But I couldn't. I couldn't tell her the truth. It would have been too dark, too dark – too dark altogether.

With these words Marlow finished his story.

He sat apart and silent. Nobody on board the *Nellie* moved for a time. The sky was dark and the river was black, seeming to lead into the heart of an immense darkness.

After Reading

Personal Response

1 **Which elements of a 'good story' (see page 14) do you think** *Heart of Darkness* **has? Tick (✓).**

a) ☐ Background and description.

b) ☐ Good plot with lots of action.

c) ☐ Satisfactory ending.

d) ☐ Hidden meaning and moral.

e) ☐ Convincing characters.

2 **Did you enjoy the story? Why/Why not?**

3 **This is what some critics have said about** *Heart of Darkness*:

a) 'a psychological masterpiece.'

b) 'Conrad's novel is also relevant today as modern man is often displaced by war, famine and genocide.'

c) 'Conrad was a racist.'

d) '…a dream of self-discovery.'

Which comments do you agree with? Which do you disagree with? Give reasons.

After Reading

Comprehension

1 Tick (✓) true (T) or false (F). Correct the false sentences.

	T	F
a) Marlow is in France when he begins to tell his story.	☐	☐
b) Marlow's new job for a trading company takes him to Africa.	☐	☐
c) His first impressions of Africa are negative.	☐	☐
d) He is in Africa to bring back sugar.	☐	☐
e) He hears many stories about a man named Kurtz.	☐	☐
f) Nobody seems to like Kurtz.	☐	☐
g) Meeting Kurtz becomes Marlow's main goal.	☐	☐
h) In the end Kurtz leaves the jungle with Marlow.	☐	☐

2 Complete the sentences with the words and expressions from the box.

> admired   girlfriend   broke down
> ill   journalist   papers

a) Marlow's steamer .... at the beginning and at the end of his journey on the river.

b) Marlow met a lot of people on his expedition but only .... Kurtz.

c) Kurtz was very .... when Marlow finally met him.

d) Kurtz was said to have many careers. He was even a ....

e) Before dying Kurtz gave Marlow a photograph and some ....

f) Marlow took a packet of things to Kurtz's ....

3 **Put these scenes from the story in chronological order.**

4 **Write a couple of sentences to describe each scene. Include: the place, the people, what's happening, etc.**

5 **Who says these things? Match the sentences with the character.**

a) 'The horror! The horror!'

Marlow

b) 'Oh, Kurtz will go very far… he will become important in the administration before long.'

Kurtz

c) 'What a loss to me – to us – to the world!'

The accountant

d) 'I think Kurtz is a remarkable man.'

Kurtz's girlfriend

6 **Put the quotations in context. When were these things said? To whom?**

After Reading

Characters

1 Complete the sentences about Marlow and Kurtz with the words from the box.

> adventure   dark   loyal   trading
> sent   sail   natives   Africa

a) He liked ………….. and was attracted to ………….. .

b) He saw it first as a map of a big ………….. area near the equator with a huge river in its centre.

c) He got a job for a ………….. company and had to ………….. down the Congo River.

d) He was ………….. to bring back Kurtz.

e) His journey was difficult and his boat was even attacked by ………….. .

f) He remained ………….. to Kurtz to the last.

> tribe   respected
> mystery   focus

g) There is a lot of ………….. surrounding his character.

h) Marlow's meeting with him soon becomes the main ………….. of the story.

i) Marlow understands that Kurtz is ………….. by everyone.

j) When Marlow finally meets him he sees he is living with a ………….. .

2 **Kurtz is a contradictory character. Read these sentences and discuss the following in groups.**

a) Do you think Kurtz was helping the African people or using them?

b) Was Kurtz a hero or a madman?

Kurtz says:

Each station must be like a light on the road to better things. A centre for trade, of course, but also for improving the natives and instructing them.

The only way to stop the traditions was to exterminate all the natives.

Kurtz

Marlow says about Kurtz:

Marlow

It had become my job not to betray Kurtz. I have remained loyal to Kurtz to the last.

Kurtz's soul was mad. Being alone in the wilderness … it had gone mad.

3 **Go back to page 6. How was Marlow similar to Conrad?**

After Reading

Plot and Theme

1 The story looks at the theme of the 'coloniser or exploiter'. Match a sentence from Box A with its corresponding quote from Box B.

A a) ☐ The people in Africa need to be educated.

b) ☐ Stealing the land from those who are different to us.

c) ☐ England was also once colonised.

B 1 The Romans first came to London … they were conquerors. They just took what they could get.

2 Going out to Africa to help those ignorant millions change their horrible ways and bring them civilisation.

3 Conquest is not a nice thing when you look at it too closely: it is robbery and murder on a large scale.

2 What view does Conrad give of Africa and the coloniser? Find examples in the story and fill in the table below.

View of Africa	....
	....
View of the coloniser	....
	....

3 **Kurtz's last words, and the most famous words of the novel are:** '*The horror! The horror!*' **In groups of four discuss what you think Kurtz was referring to.**

4 **Another theme in the story is that of the journey and how it can change us. Answer the following questions.**

a) What is the exact journey that Marlow goes on?

b) What did Marlow see in Africa that changed him?

c) How was Kurtz changed by Africa? How was he living when Marlow found him?

5 **The narrator is the person who tells the story. Who are the narrators in *Heart of Darkness*? Tick (✓).**

a) ☐ Marlow.

b) ☐ Marlow and Kurtz.

c) ☐ One of the friends on the *Nellie* and Marlow.

d) ☐ Kurtz and one of the friends on the *Nellie*.

6 **Conrad uses a frame narrative for Marlow to tell his story. This means it is a story within a story and it begins and ends on the boat, the *Nellie*, in London. What effect does this have on the reader? Tick (✓).**

a) ☐ It makes the reader feel he/she has been on a journey.

b) ☐ It makes the story seem longer.

c) ☐ It makes Africa seem very far.

After Reading

1 Complete the sentences with one of the two words below.

> dark   darkness

a) The air was ...., and there was a great gloom all over the city.

b) It was a map of a big .... area near the equator with a huge river in its centre.

c) The .... green jungle was almost black beside the glittering sea.

d) For me we were crawling towards Kurtz – exclusively, as we penetrated further and further into the heart of ....

e) What powers of .... had taken him?

f) The brown current ran out of the heart of ...., carrying us down towards the sea with twice the speed of our upward progress.

2 Darkness is the strongest symbol in the story.

> **symbol:** something that represents or stands for something else, usually by association

What do you think darkness symbolises in *Heart of Darkness*? Choose.

a) ☐ the jungle

b) ☐ the negative side of man's character

c) ☐ the natives

d) ☐ Africa

e) ☐ aspects of colonisation

f) ☐ night

3 **Our daily lives are full of symbols. Look at the following symbols and write below each one what they represent.**

> escalator   turn on/off   nuclear energy
> power   the weather   interconnection

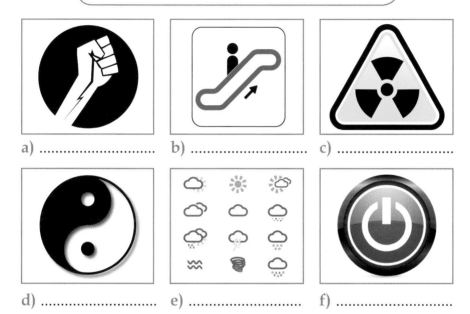

a) ....

b) ....

c) ....

d) ....

e) ....

f) ....

4 **The story takes place on a river. Use these words to complete the sentences below.**

> up river   anchored   down river   bank   current

a) We were sitting on the *Nellie*; a sailing boat. We were .... in the Thames in London.

b) It's difficult and dangerous to swim in this river as the .... is so strong.

c) I believed that the jungle on either .... was impenetrable.

d) We left the port and sailed .... as we wanted to see the countryside.

e) If we keep on travelling .... we'll soon reach the sea.

After Reading

🎧 1 **Listen and tick (✓) the correct picture.**

P 2 **Choose the correct answer.**

a) The main story is told by…
☐ Kurtz   ☐ Marlow
☐ the accountant   ☐ Kurtz's girlfriend

b) Who helped Marlow get his job with the trading company?
☐ his girlfriend   ☐ his aunt
☐ Kurtz   ☐ the owner of the company

c) What position is he given in the company?
☐ accountant   ☐ sailor
☐ mechanic   ☐ captain

d) Marlow's adventure takes place on…
☐ the Congo River   ☐ the Amazon River
☐ the Thames   ☐ the Nile

e) Marlow's first impression of Africa is…
☐ negative   ☐ positive
☐ confused   ☐ idealised

f) What does his company bring back from Africa?
☐ gold   ☐ tobacco   ☐ sugar   ☐ ivory

g) What is unusual about the crew of Marlow's boat?
☐ they are Russian   ☐ they can't speak English
☐ they are French   ☐ they are all cannibals

h) Who is the most successful trader in the company?
☐ Kurtz   ☐ the owner   ☐ the Russian   ☐ Marlow

i) Why is Marlow told to bring Kurtz back?
☐ because he's dangerous ☐ because he's ill
☐ because he's mad   ☐ because he's a criminal

j) What do the natives think about Kurtz?
☐ they think he's a god   ☐ they are afraid of him
☐ they don't like him   ☐ they are indifferent

After Reading

Projects

WEB 1 Here is an image of the British Empire when Conrad wrote *Heart of Darkness*. Do some research and find out which countries were governed by Britain; when the Empire ended; who was king/queen during this period.

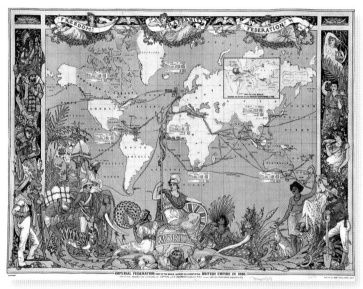

2 Interview with Marlow. Marlow has just returned from Africa. You have been asked by your local newspaper to interview him. Prepare some questions using:
- When?
- Who?
- What?
- Where?
- Why?
- How?

Work with a partner and take it in turns to ask and answer each other's questions.